Dear Parents and Educators,

Welcome to Penguin Young Readers! As parents and educators, you know that each child develops at his or her own pace—in terms of speech, critical thinking, and, of course, reading. Penguin Young Readers recognizes this fact. As a result, each Penguin Young Readers book is assigned a traditional easy-to-read level (1–4) as well as a Guided Reading Level (A–P). Both of these systems will help you choose the right book for your child. Please refer to the back of each book for specific leveling information. Penguin Young Readers features esteemed authors and illustrators, stories about favorite characters, fascinating nonfiction, and more!

The Buzz on Insects

LEVEL 3

GUIDED
READING
LEVEL **K**

This book is perfect for a **Transitional Reader** who:
• can read multisyllable and compound words;
• can read words with prefixes and suffixes;
• is able to identify story elements (beginning, middle, end, plot, setting, characters, problem, solution); and
• can understand different points of view.

Here are some **activities** you can do during and after reading this book:
• Creative Writing: Imagine you are one of the insects in this book. What do you look like? What makes you like other insects? What makes you different?
• Venn Diagram: In this book, we learn that both ants and caterpillars are types of insects. Think about how the two are alike and how they are different. Then, on a separate piece of paper, draw a Venn diagram—two circles which overlap. Label one circle "Ants" and the other circle "Caterpillars." Write the traits that are specific to each animal in the parts of the circles that don't touch. Write the traits they share in the space where the circles overlap.

Remember, sharing the love of reading with a child is the best gift you can give!

—Bonnie Bader, EdM
  Penguin Young Readers program

*Penguin Young Readers are leveled by independent reviewers applying the standards developed by Irene Fountas and Gay Su Pinnell in *Matching Books to Readers: Using Leveled Books in Guided Reading*, Heinemann, 1999.

For Jeff—thanks for all of our wonderful
outdoor trips together—bugs and all!—GS

PENGUIN YOUNG READERS
An Imprint of Penguin Random House LLC

⊛ Smithsonian

This trademark is owned by the Smithsonian Institution and
is registered in the U.S. Patent and Trademark Office.

Smithsonian Enterprises:
Christopher Liedel, President
Carol LeBlanc, Senior Vice President, Education and Consumer Products
Brigid Ferraro, Vice President, Education and Consumer Products
Ellen Nanney, Licensing Manager
Kealy Gordon, Product Development Manager

Smithsonian's National Museum of Natural History:
Gary Hevel, Emeritus Public Information Officer, Department of Entomology

Photo credits: DK Images: page 29 (thorn bug © Frank Greenaway). National Museum of Natural
History, Smithsonian: pages 1, 2, 3, 4, 8 (spider), 9, 10, 11, 12, 13, 14 (ant colony, leaf-cutter ants), 16, 17,
18 (bee), 23 (walking stick), 25 (grasshopper), 26 (stink bug, stink ant), 28 (giant stick insect), 29 (honey
bees), 30, 32. Thinkstock: cover © Peter Flyer, pages 6 (© JHVEPhoto), 7 (caterpillars © Artesia Wells,
wasps © Pacotoscano, pond skaters © Mark Mirror), 8 (worm © K. Kucharska and D. Kucharski, ticks
© Erik Karits, snails © abadonian), 14 (ant eggs © benedamiroslav), 15 (worker ants © Dariusz Majgier,
anthill © Sandra Henderson), 18 (honey bee © Sumiko Photo), 19 (ladybug © Joseph Calev, wasp
© Jeff Sinnock), 20 (© Patipas, inset © Nagydodo), 21, 22 (© Henrik Larsson), 23 (leaf insect © Danish
Khan, grasshopper © Debra Rade, dragonfly © Hugh MacDougall), 25 (cricket © vnlit), 27 (ladybug
© Paul Grecaud, stink beetle © kojihirano), 28 (Goliath beetle © Hemera Technologies), 31 (© -slav-).

Library of Congress Cataloging-in-Publication Data is available.

ISBN 978-0-448-49022-9 (pbk)   10 9 8 7 6 5 4 3 2 1
ISBN 978-0-448-49023-6 (hc)   10 9 8 7 6 5 4 3 2 1

☀ Smithsonian

The Buzz on Insects

by Gina Shaw

Penguin Young Readers
An Imprint of Penguin Random House

Contents

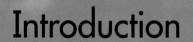

Introduction

There are many, many more insects
in the world than people.
For every person on earth, there
may be 200 million insects.
That's a lot of insects!
Insects live almost everywhere:
trees, mountains, deserts, lakes,
and under the ground.

caterpillars

wasps

butterflies

pond skaters

7

What Is an Insect?

The world is full of bugs.

But not all bugs are insects.

Spiders, worms, ticks, and snails are

bugs but not insects.

spider

worm

ticks

snails

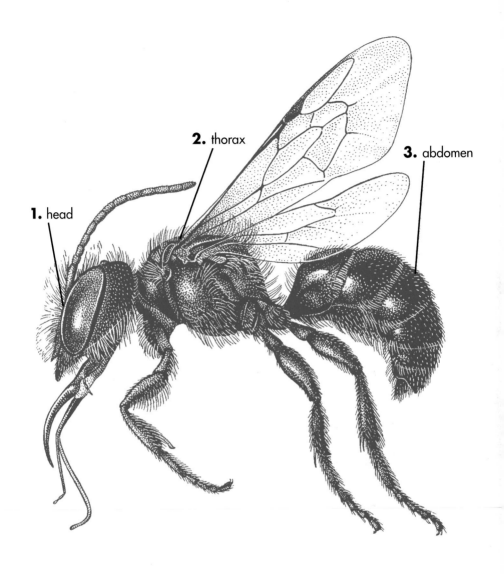

1. head

2. thorax

3. abdomen

How can you tell if a bug is an insect?

An insect has three body parts.

All insects have six legs.

They are the only animals

in the world that have six legs.

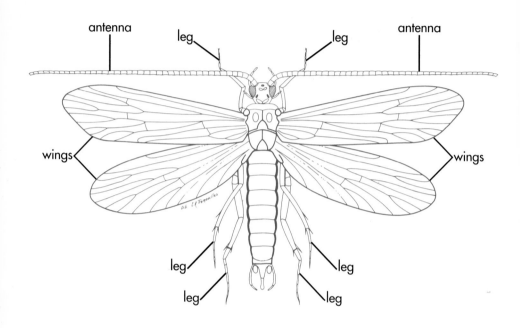

Most insects have wings and can fly.

They also have two **antennae**

on their heads.

Let's meet some insects.

dragonfly

Beetles

Beetles are the largest group of animals on earth.

They live on land and in freshwater.

Beetles come in many colors, shapes, and sizes.

different beetles

two types of Hercules beetle

frog beetle

13

Ants

Ants live and work together in **colonies**. They build their nests from leaves, dirt, and wood.

leaf-cutter ants

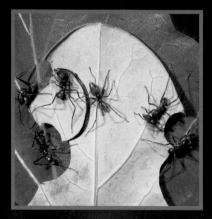

ant eggs

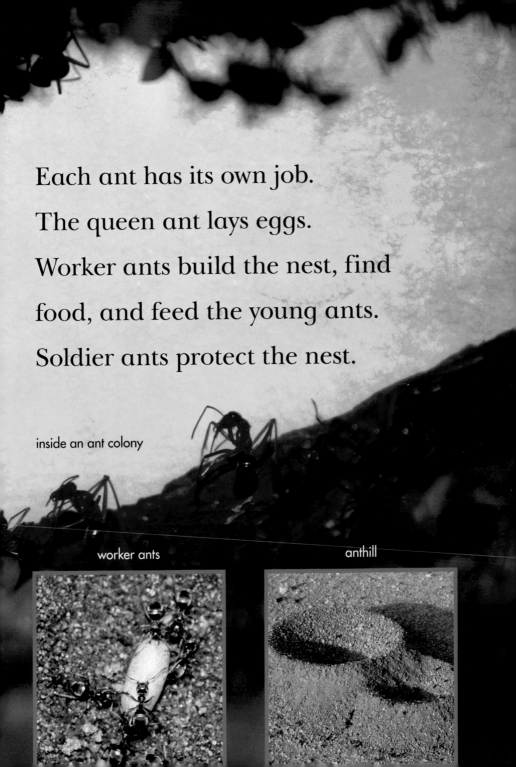

Each ant has its own job.
The queen ant lays eggs.
Worker ants build the nest, find
food, and feed the young ants.
Soldier ants protect the nest.

inside an ant colony

worker ants

anthill

Caterpillars and Then . . .

Caterpillars, like most insects,
hatch from eggs.
When they grow up, they turn into
butterflies or moths.
Most butterflies have bright colors.
They stay awake during the day.
Most moths have dull colors.
They are awake at night.

caterpillar

butterfly

caterpillar

moth

Helpful Insects

There are many helpful insects.

bee

honey bee

Bees help plants grow.

They move **pollen** from one flower to another.

Without bees, we might not have beautiful flowers.

Wasps and ladybugs are helpful, too.
Wasps feed on insects that
destroy farmers' **crops**.
Ladybugs feed on
pests that eat plants.

wasp

ladybug

Harmful Insects

Locusts are a kind of grasshopper.

They travel in large groups.

They can destroy crops.

locust

Mosquitoes are also harmful.

Female mosquitoes feed on animals and people.

Their bites can carry diseases.

mosquito

Can You Find the Insect?

Some insects are very good at blending into their **environment**. This keeps them safe from other animals that might want to eat them.

moth on rock

Can you find the
leaf insect?

Do you see the
walking stick?

Look for the
grasshopper.

Do you see the
dragonfly?

Singing Insects

Chirp. Click. Zip. Rattle.
These are sounds
that some insects make.

A male cricket chirps by rubbing
his front wings together.
Male grasshoppers rub their legs
against their wings to make sounds.

These singing insects want to attract
female **mates**.

cricket

grasshopper

Smelly Insects

Phew! Where's that yucky smell coming from? Stink bugs!

stink bug

The stink bug's bad smell warns animals that it is not good to eat. Some kinds of beetles, ladybugs, and ants also give off bad smells.

stink ant

stink beetle

ladybug

And the Winner Is . . .

Here are some facts about insects.

Giant stick insects are the longest insects.

giant stick insect

Goliath beetles are the heaviest insects.

Goliath beetle

Thorn bugs look the strangest.

thorn bug

Honey bees make honey.

They are the only insects that make

food that people can eat.

honey bees

Insects All Around

You can learn about insects
in some special places.

How about a walk through the
Butterfly Pavilion at the
Smithsonian Museum
of Natural History in
Washington, DC?

Would you like to
watch, touch, and
hold live insects at the
Smithsonian's O. Orkin Insect Zoo?

Insects are all around you.

Just keep your eyes open!

Glossary

abdomen: usually the largest part of an insect

antennae: parts on the head of an animal or insect that move and are used for touching things

colony: a large group of animals that live and work together

crop: a plant or plant product that is grown by farmers

environment: the natural world; surroundings

hatch: to come out of an egg

mate: the male or female partner in a pair of animals

pollen: a very fine yellow dust that is made by a plant and carried to other plants of the same kind by wind or insects so the plants can make seeds

thorax: the middle part of an insect where the wings and legs attach

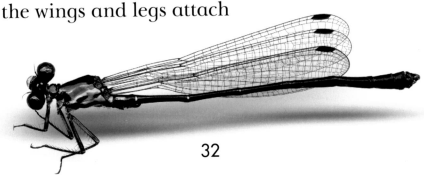